Teacher's Literacy Resource Book

Look out on the Road

by Gillian Liu

How can this resource help you in the literacy hour?

This resource provides activities to be used in the literacy hour, based upon the Rainbows title *Look out on the Road*, available as a Big Book and as a small format book. The activities are based on the common objectives set out in the National Literacy Strategy *Framework for Teaching:* comprehension and composition, grammar and punctuation, phonics, spelling and vocabulary. The sheets can be chosen to suit individual children's needs, ensuring differentiation, developing an independence in learning within the classroom organisation for a literacy hour.

The book will enable teachers to share ideas and plan activities together, encouraging continuity and consistency between classes of the same age group, and providing a focus of literacy teaching throughout the whole school, as good teaching practice demands.

It is suggested that the *Look out on the Road* Big Book be read and then used to introduce a particular concept in the whole class sessions of shared text and focused word work. The worksheets in this resource book can then be used in the group work session for independent writing or word work to reinforce specific skills and to allow teacher assessment of pupils' understanding of the points covered in the initial whole class session. The small format *Look out on the Road* books can then be used for guided reading and comprehension tasks. The final whole class session provides a further opportunity to review pupils' grasp of particular points, and through discussion to widen the scope of subjects raised by *Look out on the Road*.

Some of the concepts covered in the sheets:

Handwriting practice	worksheet 1
Letter blends	worksheet 2
Writing instructions	worksheets 3, 4 and 8
ing endings	worksheet 5
Initial sounds	worksheets 6, 10, 13 and 16
Speech marks	worksheet 7
Matching word to picture	worksheets 11 and 14
Jumbled letters	worksheet 12
Upper and lower case letters	worksheets 14 and 15
Sentence structure	worksheet 17
Labelling and answering questions	worksheets 9 and 18
Reading comprehension	worksheet 19
Fact-finding	worksheet 20

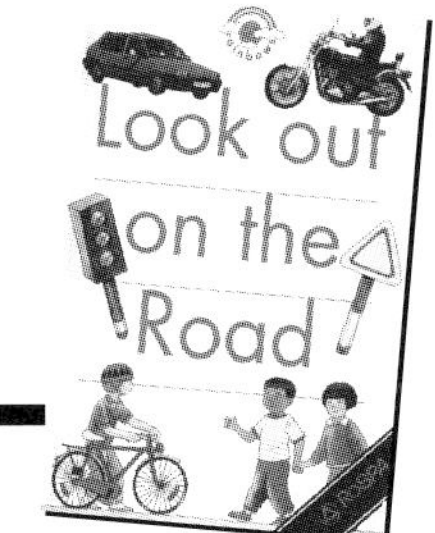

1 name

Practise your handwriting.
Draw over the road markings.

School keep clear

Bus Stop

Traffic light words

How many 3 letter words can you make on the traffic lights using **an** and **at** letter blends?

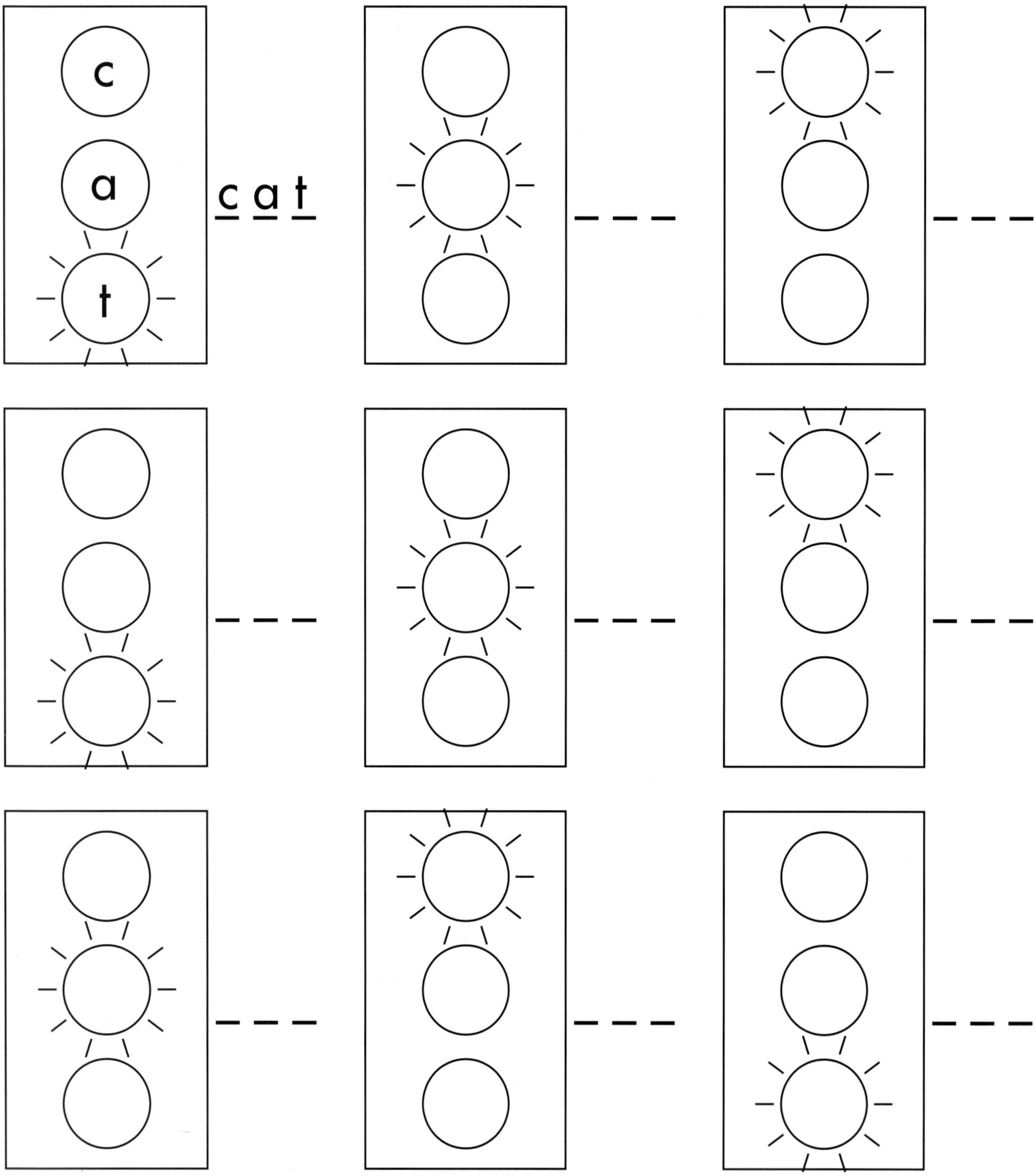

c
a
t

<u>c a t</u>

 **3**  name

straight on

turn left

turn right

roundabout

tunnel

bridge

no entry

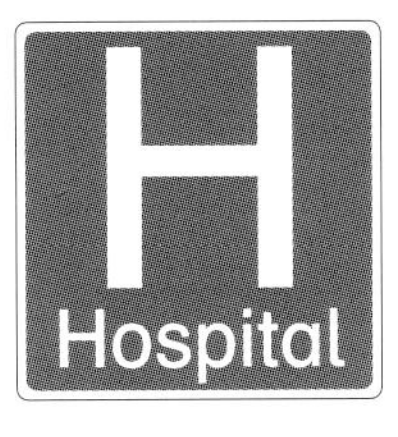

1 Draw an imaginary map from your house to your school.

2 Cut out and stick these road signs on to your map.

3 Describe your journey on a separate sheet.

4 name

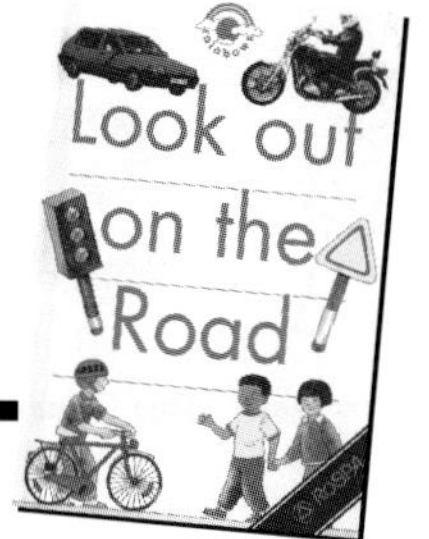

The Green Cross Code tells us how we can cross the road safely.

Stop　　　**look**　　　**listen**

Can you use these 3 words to tell a friend how to cross the road safely?

First find ....

....

....

....

....

....

....

....

5 name

A zebra crossing is a safe place to cross a road.
Add 'ing' to these words on the zebra cross<u>ings</u>
to make new words.

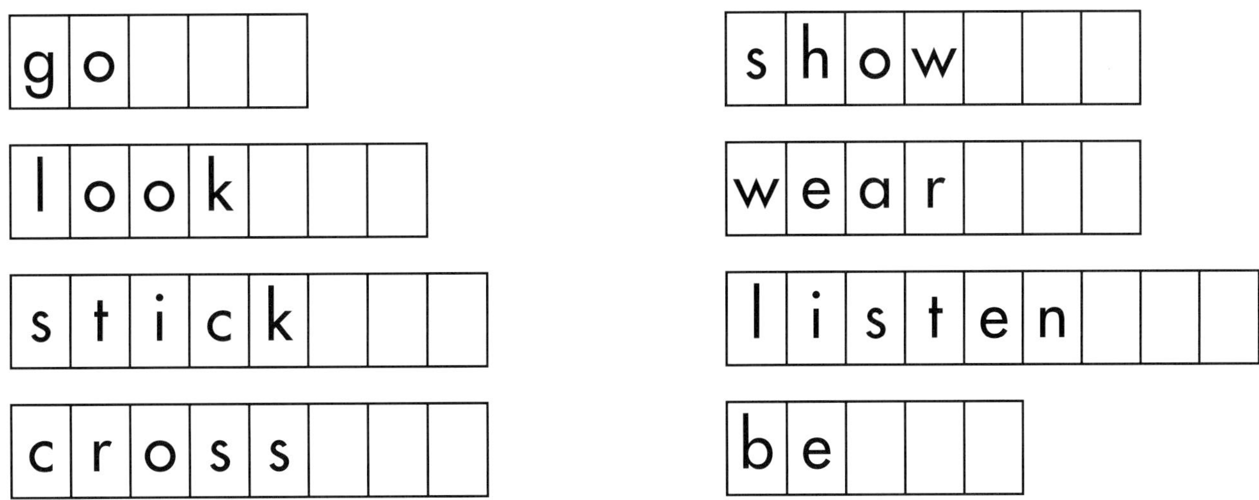

Can you write down the page numbers where we
can find these 'ing' words in the *Look out on the
road* book?

going   – page number ☐ and ☐

looking   – page number ☐ and ☐

showing   – page number ☐ and ☐

sticking   – page number ☐ and ☐

wearing   – page number ☐ and ☐

listening – page number ☐ and ☐

6   name

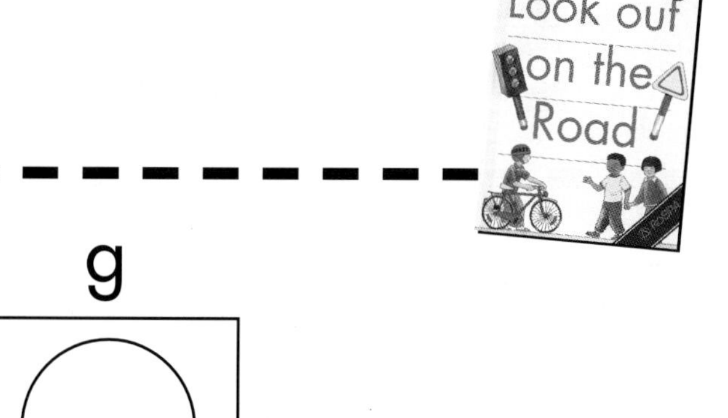

r

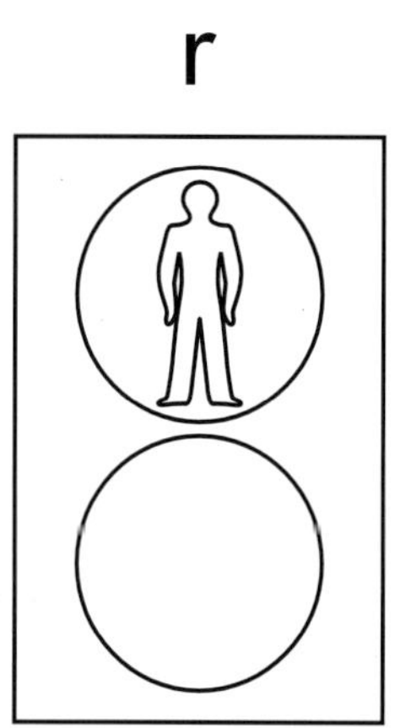
red

g

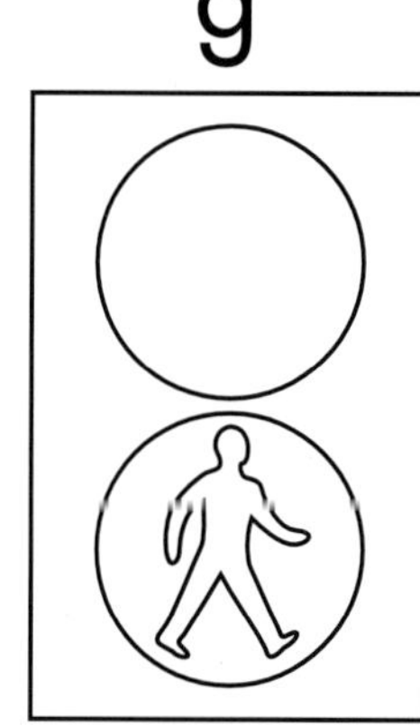
green

How many words can you find in a dictionary that begin with the letters **r** or **g**? Write some of them down.

r	g
. . . .	. . . .
. . . .	. . . .
. . . .	. . . .
. . . .	. . . .
. . . .	. . . .
. . . .	. . . .
. . . .	. . . .
. . . .	. . . .
. . . .	. . . .

7

name

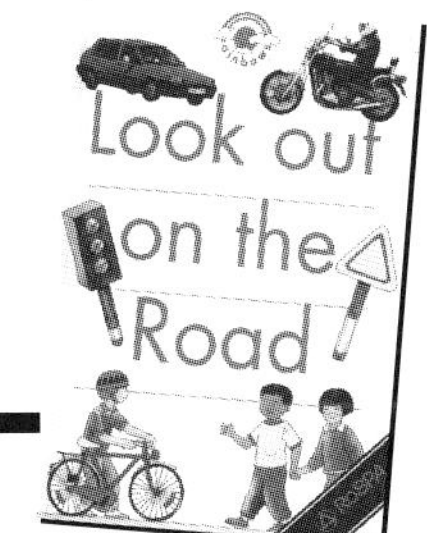

Speech marks are used to show us
when someone is talking.   "Hello."

Change these speech bubbles
into speech marked sentences.

. . . .
. . . .

. . . .
. . . .

. . . .
. . . .

. . . .
. . . .

. . . .
. . . .

. . . .
. . . .

. . . .
. . . .

 **8**  name

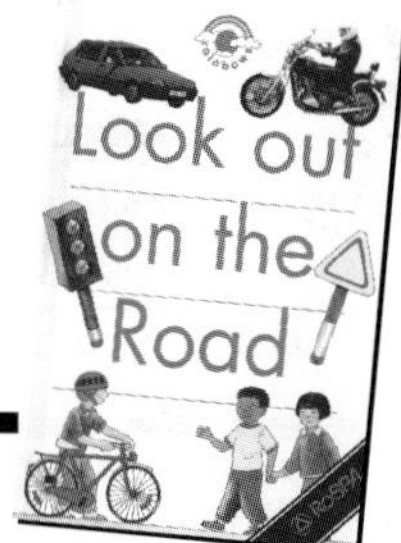

Crossing the road safely

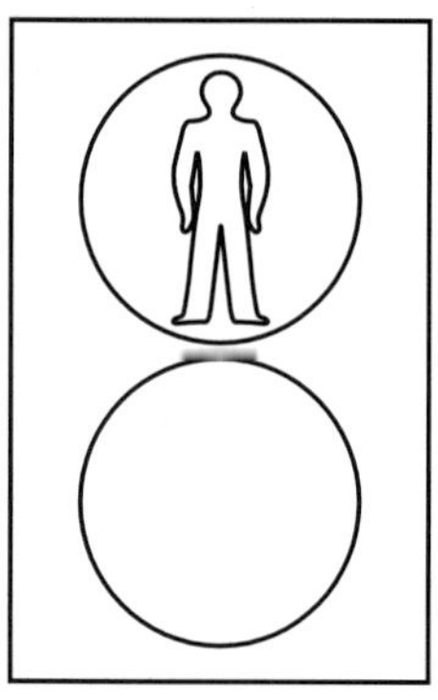

Wait

cross with
care

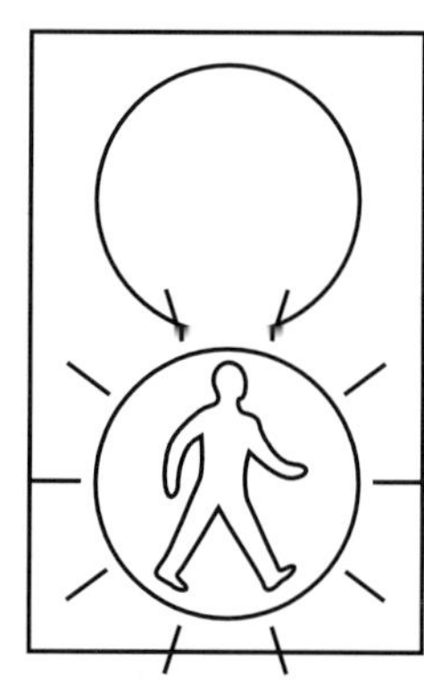

do not start
to cross

Can you tell this Space Alien how to cross the road
safely using a pelican crossing?

9 name

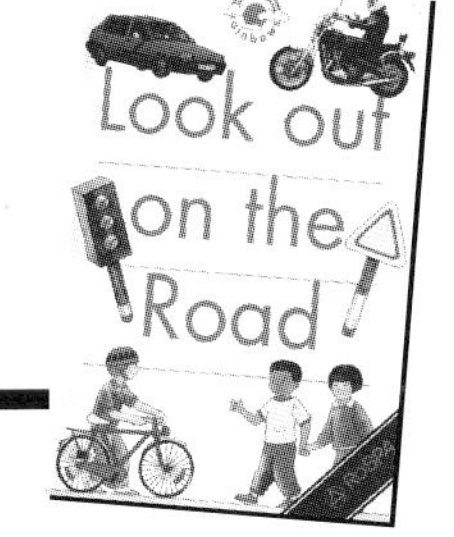

Look at the different shops.

Can you put the correct name above each shop?

| greengrocer | fishmonger | butcher |

| baker | chemist |

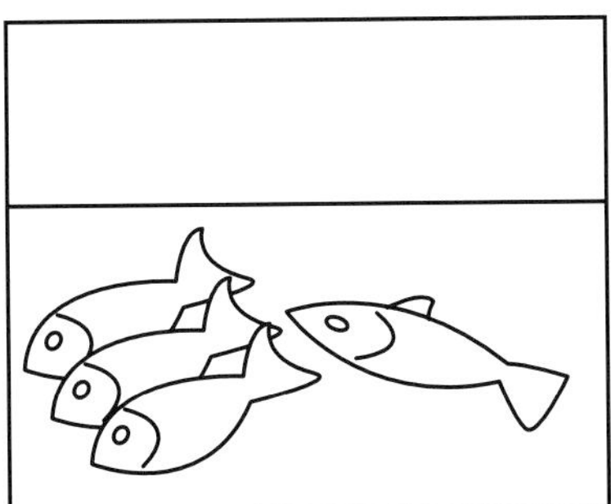

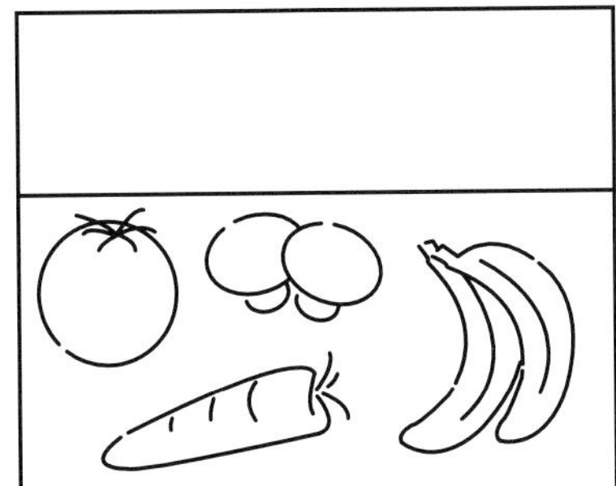

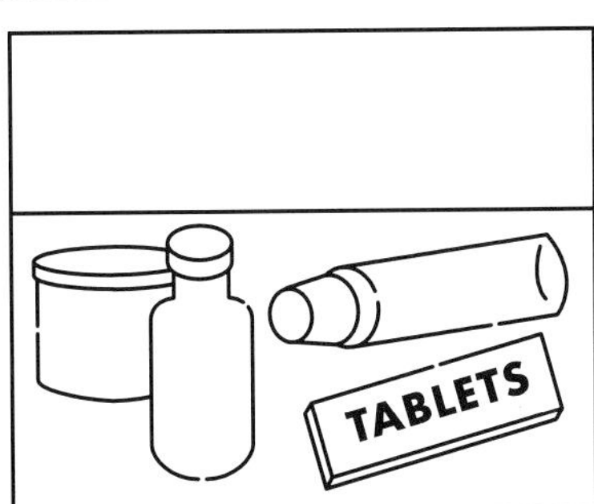

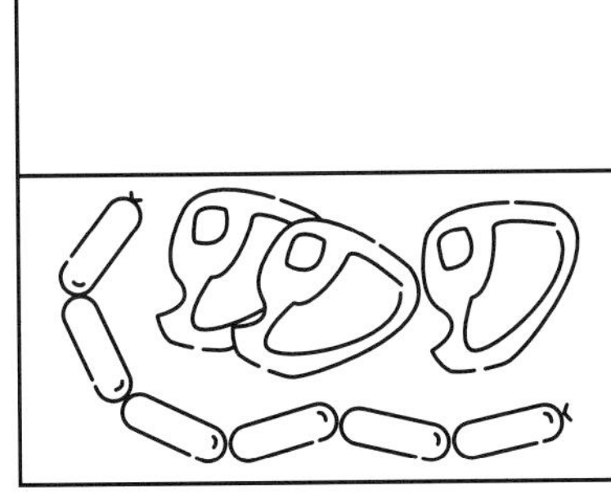

What can you buy at these shops?

At the fishmonger I can buy . . . .

At the greengrocer I can buy . . . .

At the chemist I can buy . . . .

At the baker I can buy . . . .

At the butcher I can buy . . . .

10

Wheel word game

You will need: a dice with numbers 1, 2 and 3
a counter
a pencil and paper
Look out on the road book

How to play:
Put the counter on start.
Shake the dice.
If you shake 1, move on 1 wheel along the road.
If you shake 2, move on 2 wheels along the road.
If you shake 3, move on 3 wheels along the road.

Each time you land on a letter, write down a word from the story that begins with the same sound.

letter sound	word from the story
. . . .	. . . .
. . . .	. . . .
. . . .	. . . .
. . . .	. . . .
. . . .	. . . .

Continued on next page ▶

10

Sheet 2   name

Wheel word game

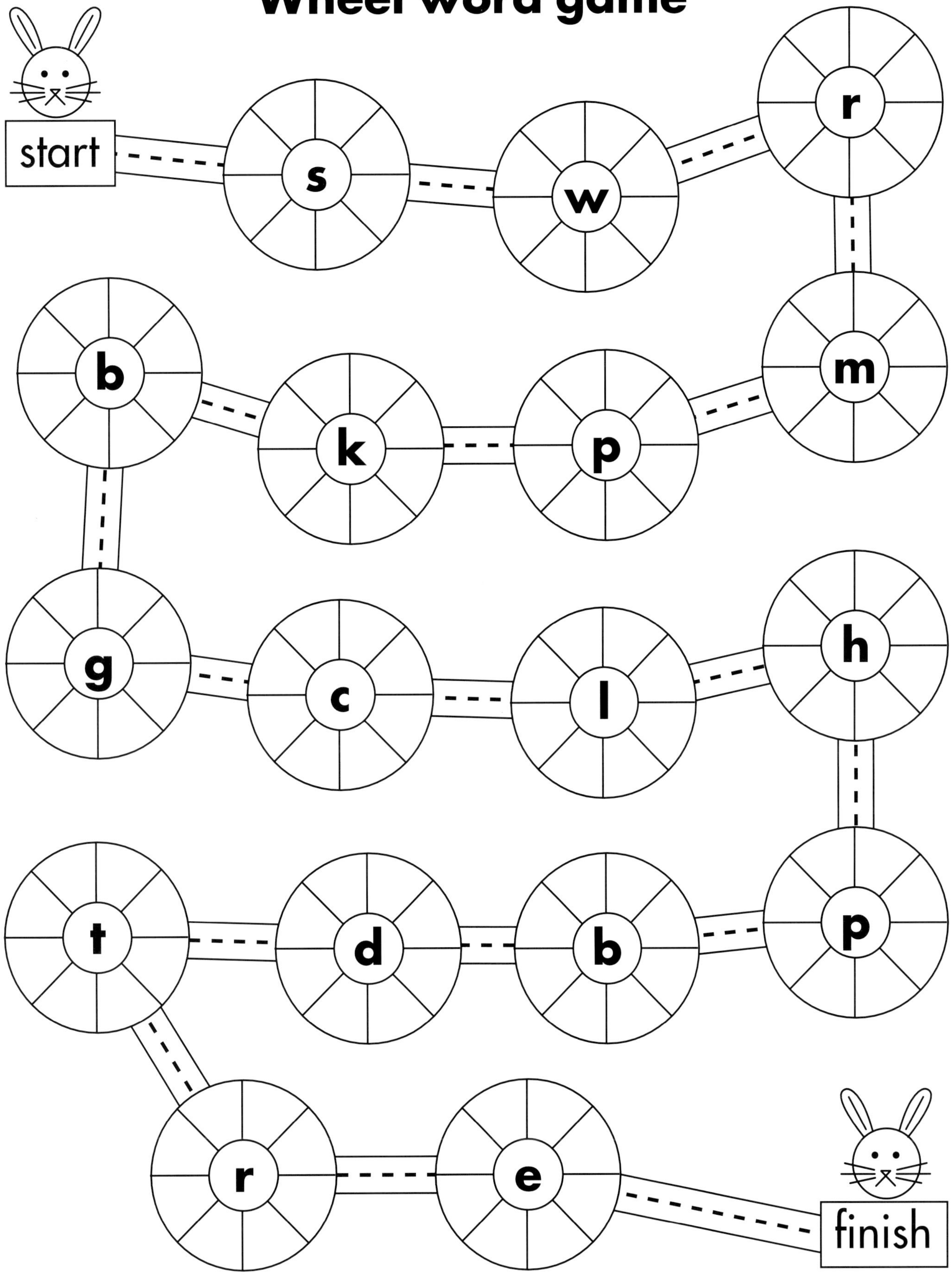

start

s

w

r

b

k

p

m

g

c

l

h

t

d

b

p

r

e

finish

a b c d e f g h i j k l m

n o p q r s t u v w x y z

Can you put the shopping in the correct trolley?

apples

jam

eggs

cake

tissues

oranges

lemons

fish

l

e

a

o

j

c

t

f

Now can you put the food in alphabetical order?

apples . . . .

. . . .

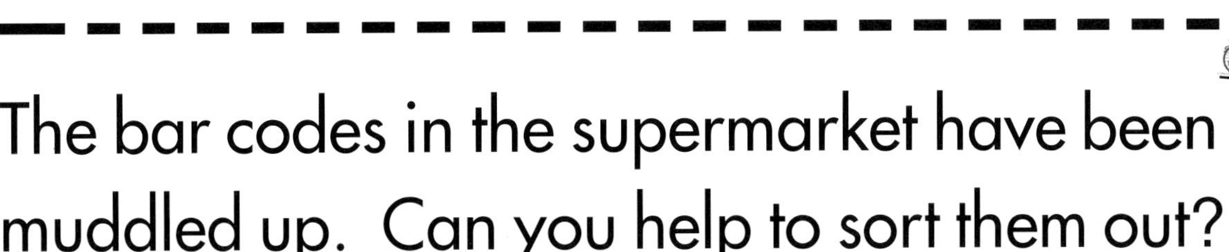

12   name

The bar codes in the supermarket have been muddled up. Can you help to sort them out?

| | | | | _ _ _ _ _
c k a e s

| | | | _ _ _ _
m a e t

| | | | | | _ _ _ _ _ _
c h s e e e

| | | | _ _ _ _
f s h i

| | | | | _ _ _ _ _
b d r e a

| | | | | _ _ _ _ _
f u i r t

| | | _ _ _
t a e

| | | | | | | _ _ _ _ _ _ _
t r l l o y e s

Now can you help to put some of the signs in the correct place in the supermarket?

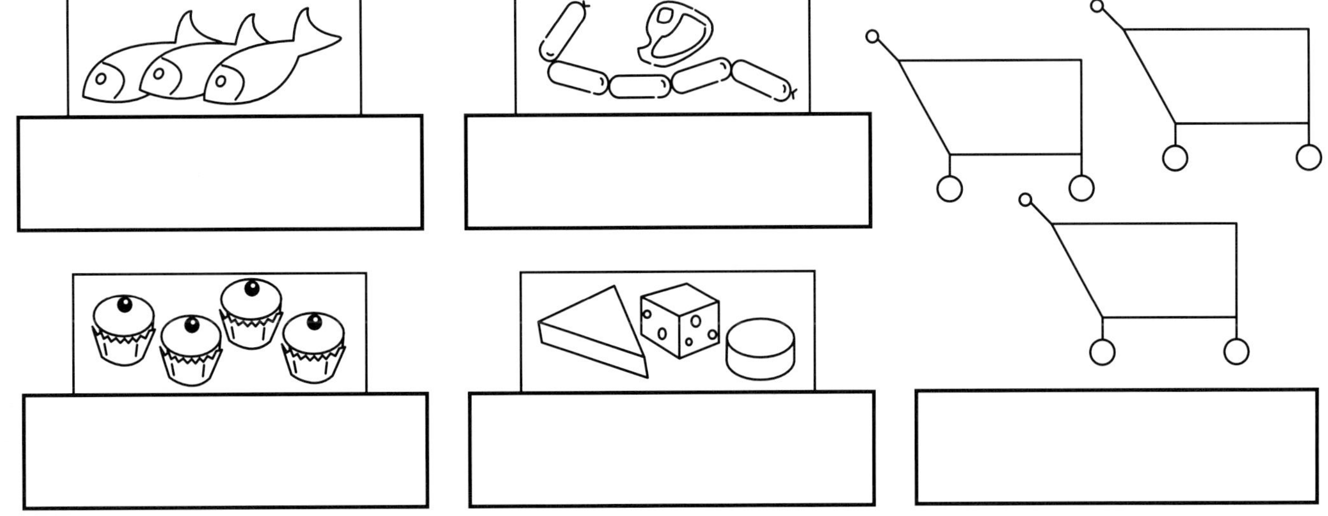

13

Sheet 1   name

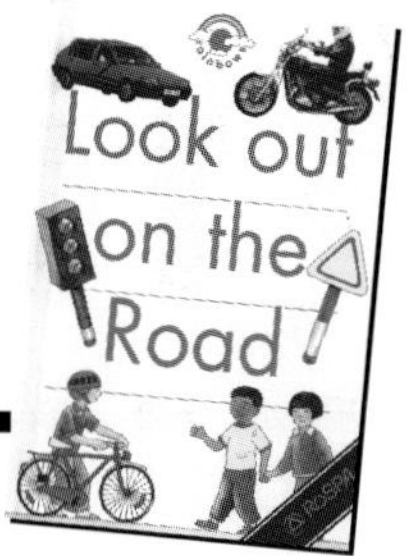

a b c d e f g h i j k l m n o p q r s t u v w x y z

Match the correct letter to the picture.

c

b

d

r

m

l

p

h

mummy

car

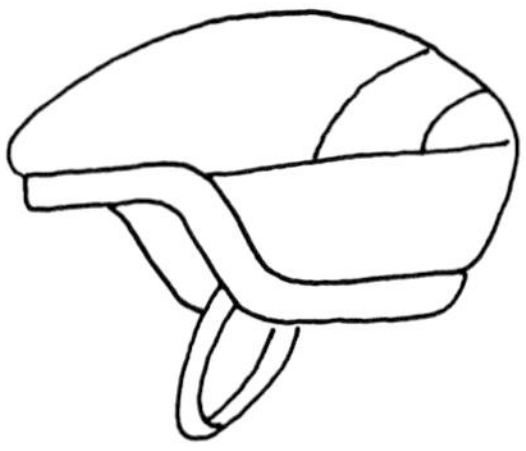

helmet

policeman

lollipop lady

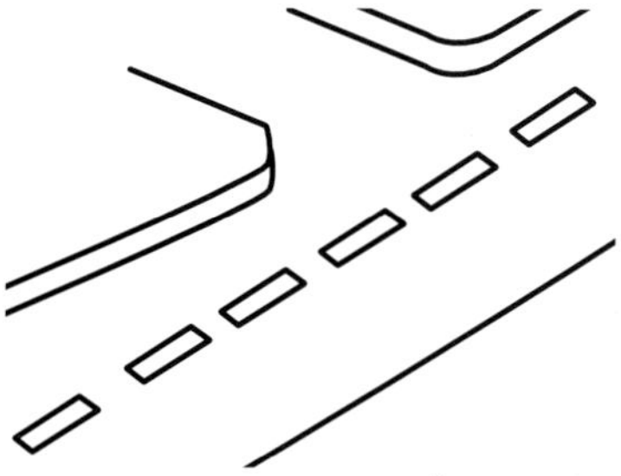

road

bus

daddy

Continued on next page ▶

13 Sheet 2   name

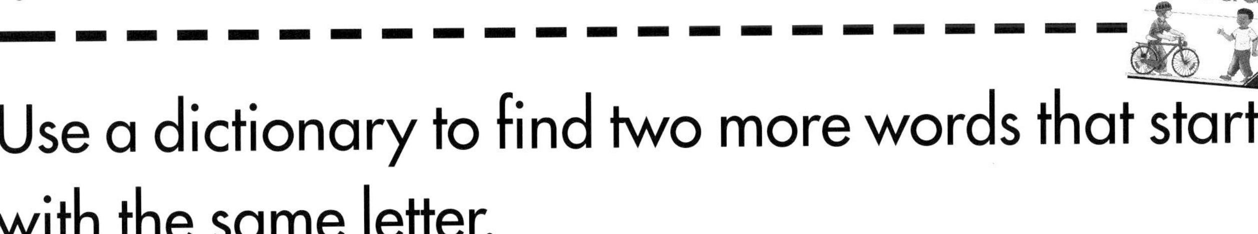

Use a dictionary to find two more words that start
with the same letter.
Write a word and draw a picture in the boxes.

car	cat	
bus		
daddy		
helmet		
road		
lollipop lady		
mummy		
policeman		

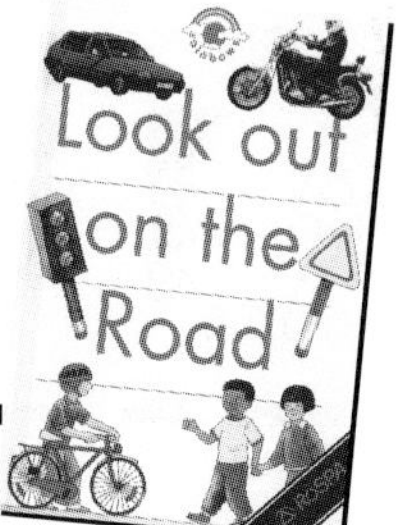

Can you write the upper case letter next to the lower case letter?

a		b		c		d		e		f		g		h
i		j		k		l		m		n		o		p
q		r		s		t		u		v		w		x
y		z												

Change the lower case letters to upper case letters at the beginning of these names.

anna		ella		william	
mary		harry		zara	
kay		jack		sam	

Now put the children's names on the bus in alphabetical order.

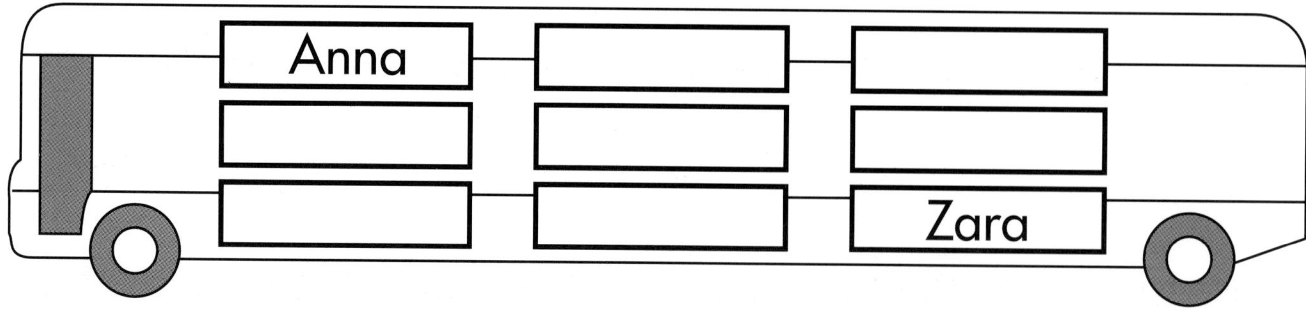

15 name

Can you write the lower case letter next to the upper case letter?

We use upper case letters at the beginning of a sentence.

A	B	C	D	E	F	G	H
I	J	K	L	M	N	O	P
Q	R	S	T	U	V	W	X
Y	Z						

Can you put in the missing upper case letters in this story?

Draw a circle around the letters that need to be changed. Write the upper case letter above the circled letter.

let's look for a safe place to cross the road. here is a

pelican crossing. now we must wait for the signal before

we cross the road. be sure to go on listening and looking

while you cross the road. there are other safe places to

cross the road. the lollipop lady at school stops the traffic.

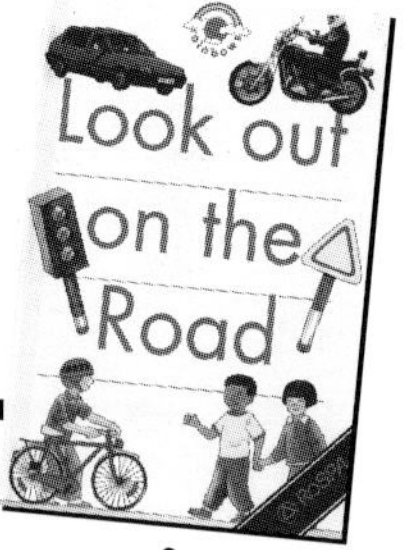

16 name

How many words can you find using the letters in some of the words from the story?

Word wheels

1 road

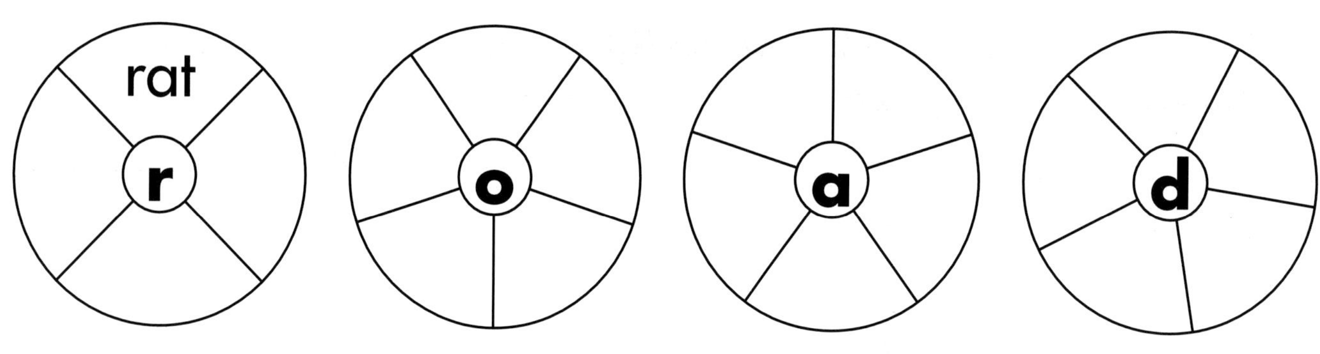

2 bus

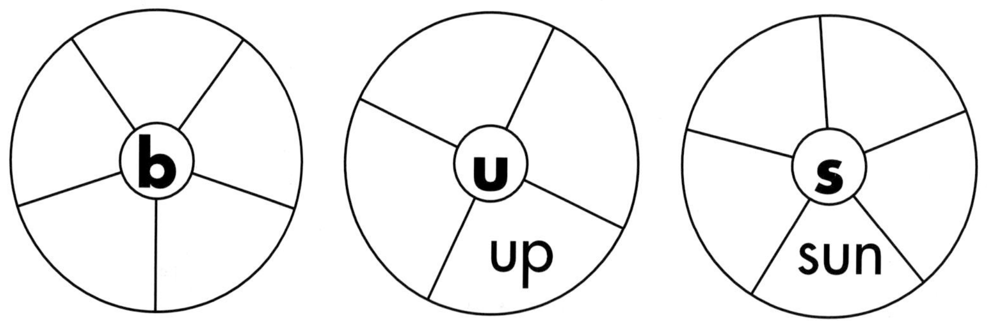

3 bike

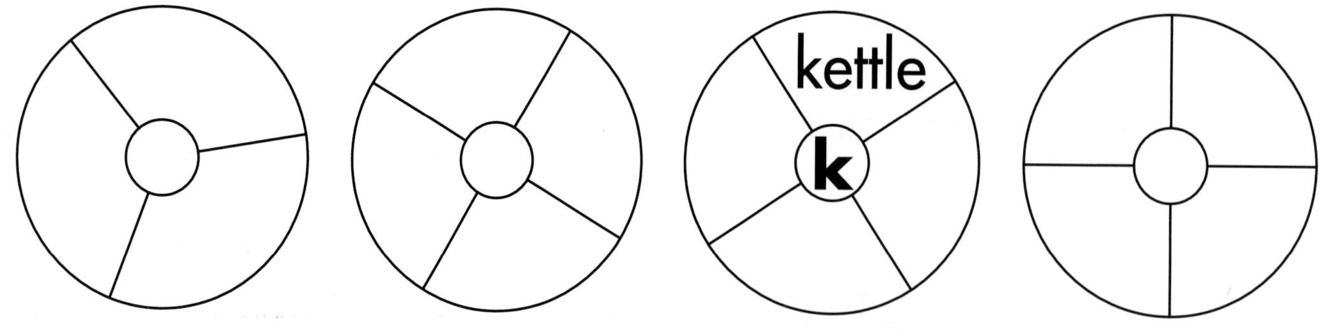

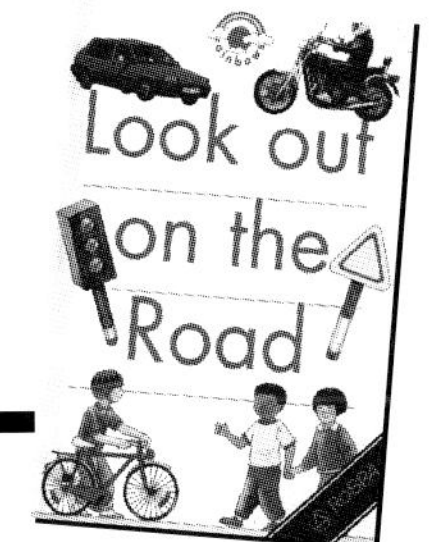

There are lots of people who help us.
The lollipop lady and the policeman help the children in the story to cross the road safely.

How do these people help us?
Write a sentence about each one.

The doctor	. . . .
The teacher	. . . .
The nurse	. . . .
The lollipop lady	. . . .
The policeman	. . . .

name

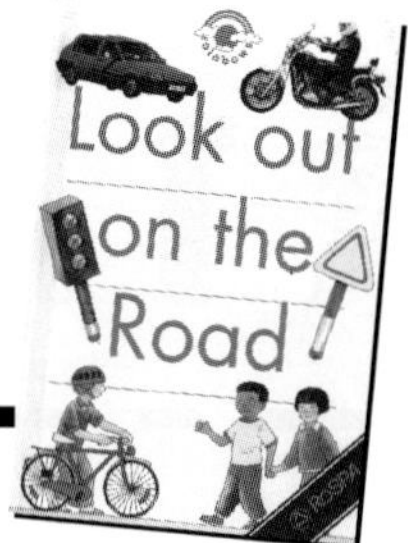

Bicycles

Can you draw a picture of a bicycle?

Can you label all the parts of the bicycle?

| saddle | handlebars | wheel | spokes |

| pedal | tyre | chain | brakes |

Why must I wear a helmet?

Why must I wear a shiny belt?

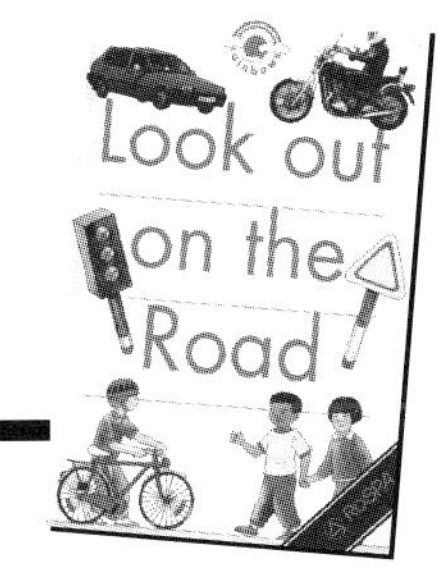

Countryside or the town?

Can you write down more differences between the countryside and the town?

countryside	town
. . . .	. . . .
. . . .	. . . .
. . . .	. . . .
. . . .	. . . .
. . . .	. . . .

Where would you like to live? . . . .

Why? . . . .

. . . .

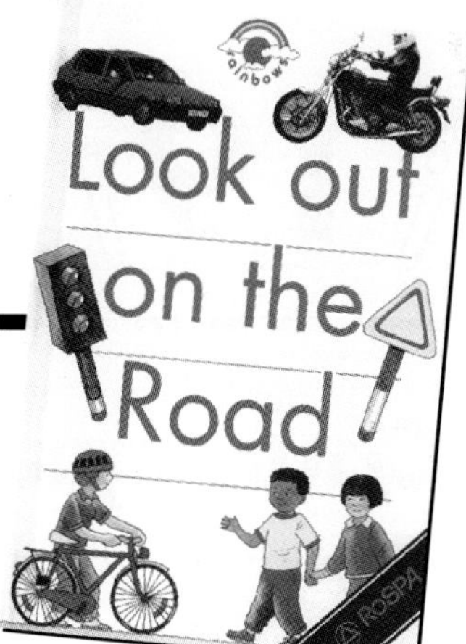

1 What is an author? . . . .
. . . .

2 What is an illustrator? . . . .
. . . .

3 What does the title of a book tell you? . . . .
. . . .

4 What is an index? . . . .
. . . .

5 Who are the authors of the book 'Look out on
the road'? . . . .

6 Who was the illustrator of the book?
. . . .

Choose 2 books and find out . . .

the title . . . .

the author . . . .

the illustrator . . . .

Make a book with a friend. Give your book a title.
Are you the author or the illustrator?